MW01073259

Who Was Galileo Galilei?

Galileo Galilei
Biography for Kids
Tanya Turner

PUBLISHED BY:

Tanya Turner

Disclaimer

The information contained in this book is for general information purposes only. The information is provided by the authors and, while we endeavor to keep the information up to date and correct, we make no representations or warranties of any kind, expressed or implied, about the completeness, accuracy, reliability, suitability or availability with respect to the book or the information, products, services, or related graphics contained in the book for any purpose. Any reliance you place on such information is therefore strictly at your own risk.

TABLE OF CONTENTS

3

ALL ABOUT GALILEO GALILEI

Who is Galileo Galilei?

Galileo Galilei, a man simply known as Galileo, was one of the most important people of science. He helped in the development of astronomy, physics, mathematics, philosophy, and more. Thanks to his great mind and the discoveries he made way before anyone else, he is considered to be the Father of Modern Science. His ideas were used later on by another great scientist, Isaac Newton, who made a huge difference in the world we live in today.

Portrait of Galileo Galilei. Justus Sustermans / <u>National Maritime Museum</u> / Public Domain

Early Life of Galileo Galilei

Galileo Galilei was born in Pisa, Italy on February 15, 1564. His father was Vincenzo Galilei, a famous musician and music teacher, and his mother was Guilia Ammanati. He was the eldest of six children.

When he was 8 years old, his family moved to Florence and left him in Pisa. He followed his family after two years and started school at the Camaldolese monastery in Vallombrosa when he was 10 years old. He was a very intelligent boy and was always curious about his surroundings.

Due to their Roman Catholic background, Galileo wanted to be a priest when he was young, but his father convinced him to become a doctor instead. So in 1581, he enrolled at the University of Pisa to study medicine.

FATHER OF MODERN SCIENCE

University Life

Galileo Galilei's first scientific observation happened while he was attending university, when he saw a chandelier swinging from the ceiling of the Cathedral of Pisa. He noticed that no matter what distance the chandelier swung, it still took the same amount of time to swing back and forth. This was very different from the scientific beliefs during that time.

The chandelier of Galileo at the
Cathedral of Pisa. © JoJan /
Wikimedia Commons / CC BY-
SA 3.0 / GFDL

Galileo accidentally attended a
geometry class, which sparked his

interest in mathematics. He asked his father to let him study mathematics and natural philosophy instead of medicine. He learned about the scientific views of the ancient Greek philosopher Aristotle, which were the only scientific beliefs allowed by the Roman Catholic Church. But because of financial problems, Galileo wasn't able to finish his studies and he left the university in 1585.

Becoming a Scientist

Being out of the university didn't stop Galileo from wanting to learn. He started to do experiments with different kinds of objects and tried to figure out how the objects moved by using mathematical equations. He invented the thermoscope, the first device to measure temperature, which was replaced by the thermometer later.

When he left the university, Galileo got teaching jobs in Florence and Siena. In 1856, he also taught at Vallombrosa and published a book called *The Little Balance,* which was about finding the gravity of an object by using a balance. This book made him known to the scientific community.

Galileo also studied fine arts. In 1588, he got a job as a teacher at Accademia delle Arti del Disegno in Florence where he taught chiaroscuro, an art technique where there is a huge difference between light and dark colors.

As Galileo's reputation continued to grow, he became the Chair of

Headquarters of the Accademia delle Arti del Disegno. © Sailko / Wikimedia Commons / CC BY 2.5 / GFDL

Mathematics at the University of Pisa in 1589. He did his experiments and made great discoveries. In 1590, he wrote *On Motion* which was about motion and falling objects. His ideas were very different from Aristotle's teachings.

In 1592, Galileo found another job at the University of Padua where he taught geometry, mechanics, and astronomy until 1610. His popularity increased because people enjoyed his lectures, and it attracted a lot of people and followers.

The Scientific Method

During the time of Galileo, people only studied what was available to them, like the works of Aristotle. There was no one who actively conducted experiments; they just believed that Aristotle's teachings were true. Galileo was different. He wanted to know more about these scientific beliefs. He wanted to observe and experience these things himself.

Galileo wasn't the first person to

have a scientific method, but he is the one who is credited with the scientific method we know today. Before Galileo, the scientific method was all about explaining why something happened. But he thought scientists should explain something with the help of mathematics, which could be used to prove it.

CONTROVERSIAL STUDIES

Tower of Pisa Experiment

When he was teaching at the University of Pisa, he did an

experiment to determine whether or not the traditional belief that when two objects of the same size but different weights are dropped, the heavier object falls to the ground first. He went on top of the Leaning Tower of Pisa and dropped two balls of the same size but different weights. The balls landed at the same time.

Galileo did more experiments. He discovered that the speed of an object isn't related to its weight. He also discovered a math equation for inertia, which is the tendency of an object to resist change in motion or rest. When

The Leaning Tower of Pisa. © W. Lloyd Mackenzie / Wikimedia Commons / CC BY-SA 3.0

you're inside a car and it suddenly brakes, your body moves forward. This is inertia. His studies were used later by Isaac Newton when he created the law of acceleration.

Most people from the university didn't like Galileo's experiments because they believed in Aristotle's ideas. This made him unpopular with the people in the University of Pisa, and this was the reason why he left. He moved to the University of Padua, where he was free to experiment and talk about his new ideas.

Telescope

In 1609, Galileo Galilei heard
about an invention from Holland
called the telescope that could
make objects from far away
appear much closer. He soon
developed his own version and
called it the perspicillum. It was an
improved version of the telescope
because it could view objects even
farther away. He began to look at
the sky, and he used it to look at
the planets and stars.

In 1610, Galileo wrote *The Starry
Messenger,* which contained his

Replica of Galileo's Telescope on display at Griffith Observatory. © Michael Dunn / <u>Wikimedia Commons</u> / <u>CC BY-SA 3.0</u> / <u>GFDL</u>

discoveries from looking at the sky with his telescope. He discovered that the moon was a sphere and had craters, which was different from the belief that the moon was flat and smooth. He also saw that Jupiter had moons that revolved around it and that there are a large number of stars in the sky.

Heliocentrism

During Galileo's time, people believed in Aristotle's ideas, and one of them was that the Earth was the center of the universe.

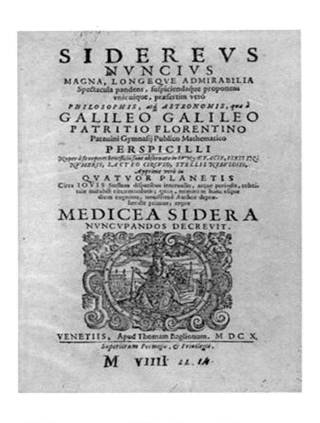

Title page of *The Starry Messenger.*

Galileo started to question Aristotle's idea when he saw different things through his telescope. He then studied Nicolaus Copernicus' heliocentric idea, which states that the Sun is the center of the universe.

In 1613, Galileo discovered that the sun has sunspots. He also discovered that Venus has phases similar to the moon, which proved that it rotates around the sun. He recorded his discoveries and published *Letters on Sunspots*. Aristotle believers and the

Catholic Church didn't like what he wrote.

Galileo wrote a *Letter to the Grand Duchess Christina* to defend heliocentrism. He said that it didn't go against the writings in the Bible and that what he wrote shouldn't be taken literally. The letter was published publicly and the Copernican theory was considered heretical because it went against what many believed at the time.

In 1616, Pope Paul V told Galileo that heliocentrism was heresy. He

LETTERA

DEL SIGNOR

GALILEO GALILEI

ACCADEMICO LINCEO.

SCRITTA ALLA

GRANDUCHESSA

DI TOSCANA.

IN CVI

Teologicamente, e con ragioni saldissime, cavate da' Padri più sen-
titi, si risponde alle calunnie di coloro, i quali a tutto potere
si sforzarono non solo di sbandirne la sua opinione in-
torno alla constituzione delle parti dell' Univer-
so, ma altresì di addurne una perpetua
infamia alla sua persona.

IN FIORENZA,
MDCCX.

Title page of Galileo's *Letter to the Grand Duchess Christina.* Theresa LaBrecque / <u>The Galileo Trial</u> / Public Domain

was not allowed to teach, talk, or write about the Copernican theory. He obeyed in order to make his life easier, and because he was also a devoted Catholic. The next pope, Pope Urban VIII, was a friend of Galileo. He allowed Galileo to write about heliocentrism, but he had to make it appear as math exercises rather than reality.

In 1632, Galileo wrote *Dialogue Concerning Two Chief World Systems*, a book defending Copernican theory and completely going

Title page of *Dialogue Concerning Two Chief World Systems*. Stefan Della Bella / Institute and Museum of the History of Science / Public Domain

against Aristotle's teachings. He was called out by the Roman Catholic Inquisition and was sentenced to life in prison. The sentence was later changed to house arrest.

GALILEO'S LATER LIFE

Galileo's Final Years

While on house arrest, Galileo Galilei stayed at his home in Arcetri, in Florence, Italy. He continued to work and wrote the *Discourses and Mathematical Demonstrations Relating to Two New Sciences,* which contained a summary of the works he did before. The *Two New Sciences* was smuggled off to Holland, where it was published because his works were not allowed in Italy. This book was highly praised by scientist Albert Einstein.

In 1638, Galileo went completely blind and encountered multiple other health problems. On January8, 1642, he died after having a fever and heart problems in Villa il Gioiello, his home in Arcetri. He wanted to be buried in his family tomb in the Basilica of

Title page of *Discourses and Mathematical Demonstrations Relating to Two New Sciences.* <ins>Posner Memorial Collection</ins> / Public Domain

Santa Croce, but the Catholic
Church didn't allow it. He was
buried in another area of the
basilica instead.

Villa il Gioiello, the last home of
Galileo. Cyberuly / Wikimedia
Commons / CC BY-SA 3.0

Legacy of Galileo Galilei

In 1737, Galileo Galilei was reburied in the main body of the Basilica of Santa Croce by the government after a monument for him was made. In 1758, works about the Copernican theory were finally allowed, and heliocentrism was fully accepted in 1835.

In the 20th century, several popes praised and supported Galileo's discoveries, but they didn't say that the Church was wrong for sentencing him. In 1992, Pope John Paul II admitted regret for

Tomb of Galileo Galilei in Basilica of Santa Croce, Florence.

how Galileo's case was handled and finally closed the case.

Galileo's discoveries and studies about the Copernican theory are very important to our understanding of the universe. Without him, we would still think that the Earth is the center of the universe. His studies also helped other scientists after him create new ideas that lead to the science we know today. Even Albert Einstein called Galileo "The Father of Modern Science," a title he greatly deserves.

Made in the
USA
Monee, IL

16029471R00024